Mazen Kerbaj

LEARNING DEUTSCH

HATJE
CANTZ

01/01

ثقب الباب

peephole

(das) Guckloch

02/01

رغوة

foam

(der) Schaum

03/01

مشط

comb

(der) Kamm

04/01

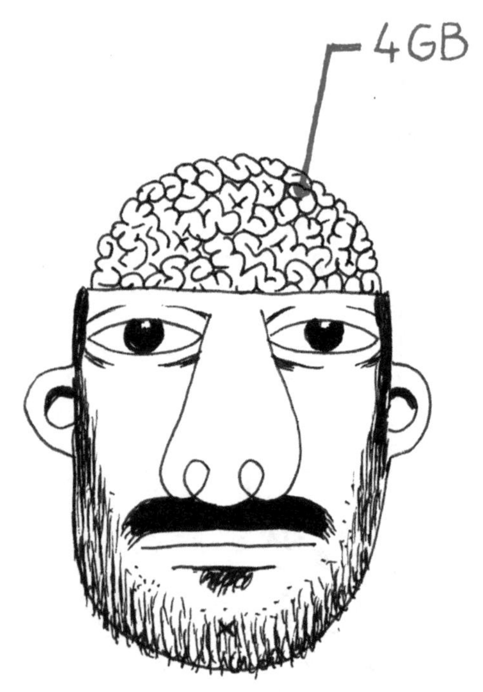

بطاقة الذاكرة

memory card

(die) Speicherkarte

05/01

برواز

frame

(der) Rahmen

06/01

غائم

cloudy

wolkig

07/01

انعكاس

mirror image

(das) Spiegelbild

08/01

شيطان

devil

(der) Teufel

09/01

متاهة

maze

(der) Irrgarten

10/01

قسطل

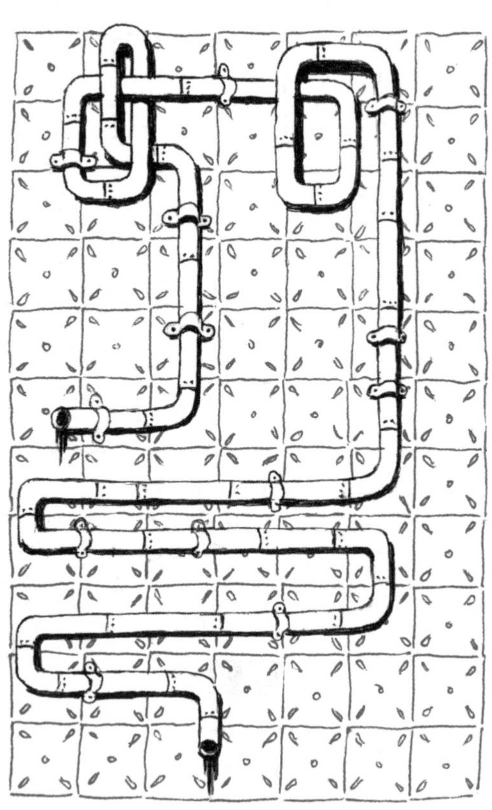

pipe

(das) Rohr

غاضب

angry

wütend

12/01

جنس

gender

(das) Geschlecht

13/01

رجفة

tremor

(das) Zittern

14/01

طريق غير نافذ

dead-end

(die) Sackgasse

أرنب

rabbit

(das) Kaninchen

طابع

stamp

(die) Briefmarke

17/01

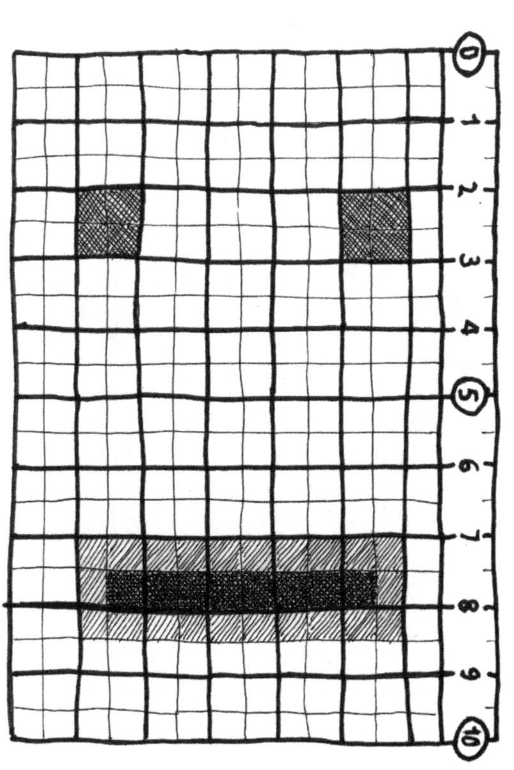

grid

شبكة

(das) Raster

18/01

شاهد القبر

gravestone

(der) Grabstein

19/01

استكشاف

exploration

(die) Erforschung

20/01

sponge

(der) Schwamm

21/01

وصلات

connections

(die) Verbindungen

22/01

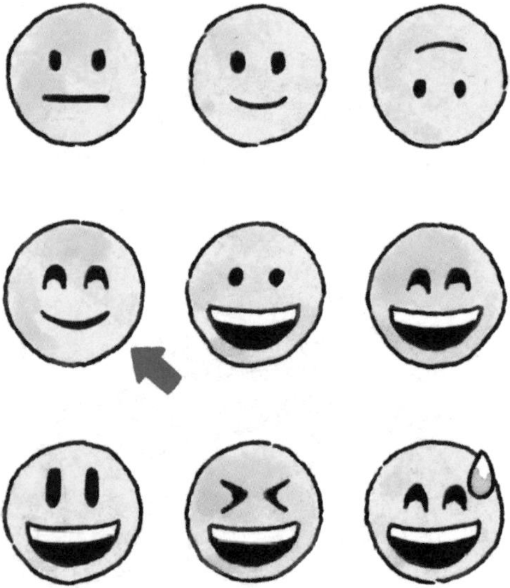

راضٍ

satisfied

zufrieden

23/01

متعدد

multiple

vielfach

24/01

power socket

(die) Steckdose

25/01

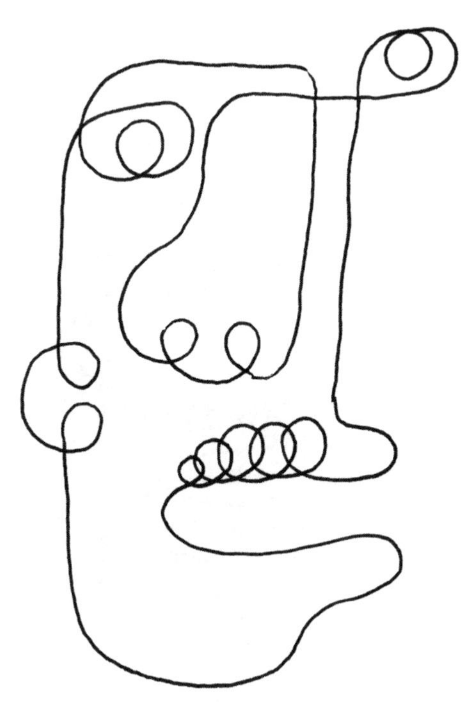

غير متقطّع

uninterrupted

ununterbrochen

26/01

مبلل

wet

nass

27/01

clothespin

(die) Wäscheklammer

28/01

خالٍ من الكحول

non-alcoholic

alkoholfrei

29/01

الطباعة بالشاشة الحريرية

screen print

(der) Siebdruck

30/01

سحّاب

zipper

(der) Reißverschluss

31/01

معاقرة الخمر

alcohol consumption

(der) Alkoholkonsum

01/02

صداع الخمر

hangover

(der) Kater

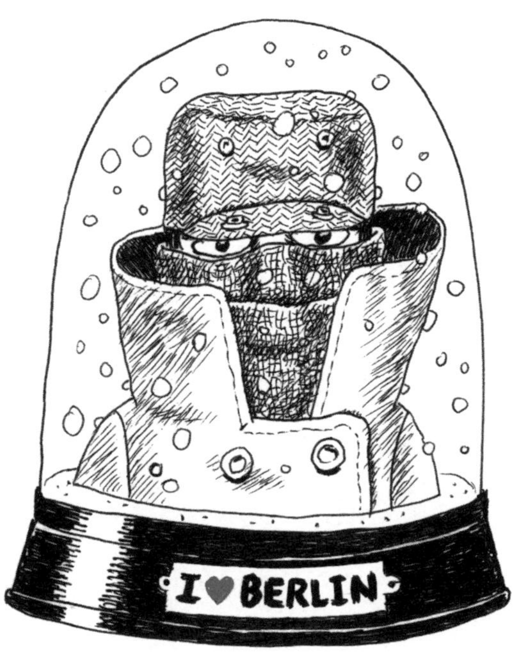

تتجمّد

to freeze

frieren

03/02

شفّاف

transparent

durchsichtig

04/02

fried eggs

(die) Spiegeleier

05/02

ظفر

fingernail

(der) Fingernagel

06/02

خربشة

scribble

(die) Kritzelei

معيل وحيد

single parent

(der) Alleinerziehende

08/02

ناقد الطعام

food critic

(der) Gastronomiekritiker

09/02

نجمة البحر

starfish

(der) Seestern

10/02

دودة الأذن

earworm

(der) Ohrwurm

11/02

شبح

ghost

(das) Gespenst

12/02

مشتبه به

suspect

(der) Verdächtige

13/02

كرنفال

carnival

(der) Fasching

14/02

مبتذل

cheesy

kitschig

15/02

طباعة شبكيّة

halftone printing

(der) Rasterdruck

16/02

أرق

insomnia

(die) Schlaflosigkeit

17/02

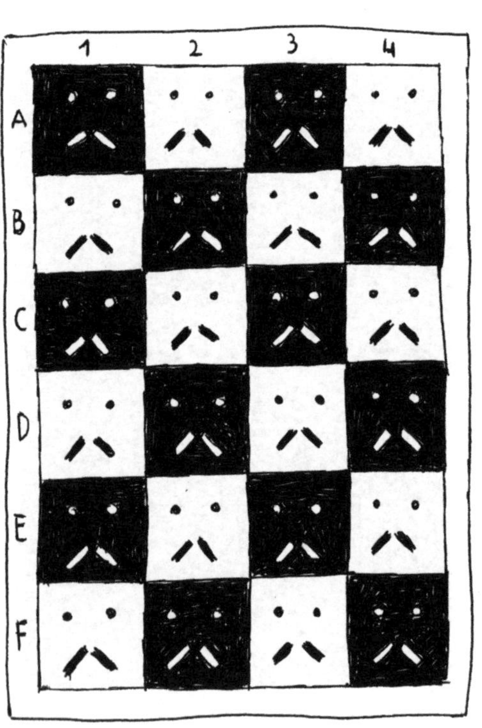

رقعة الشطرنج

chessboard

(das) Schachbrett

18/02

خجول

shy

schüchtern

19/02

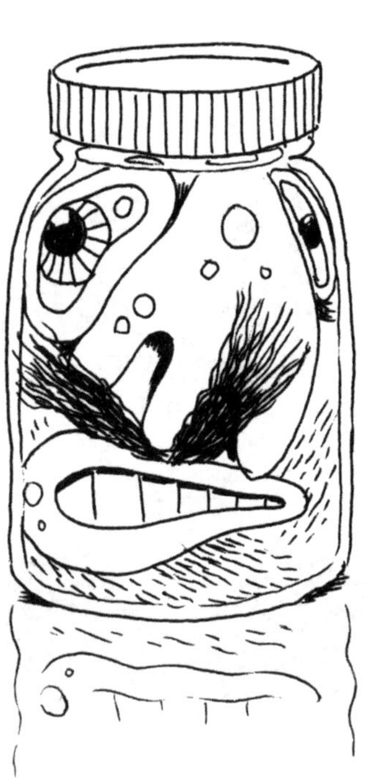

كبيس

pickles

(die) Essiggurken

20/02

استوائي

tropical

tropisch

21/02

إضاءة خلفيّة

backlighting

(das) Gegenlicht

22/02

مكسور

broken

gebrochen

23/02

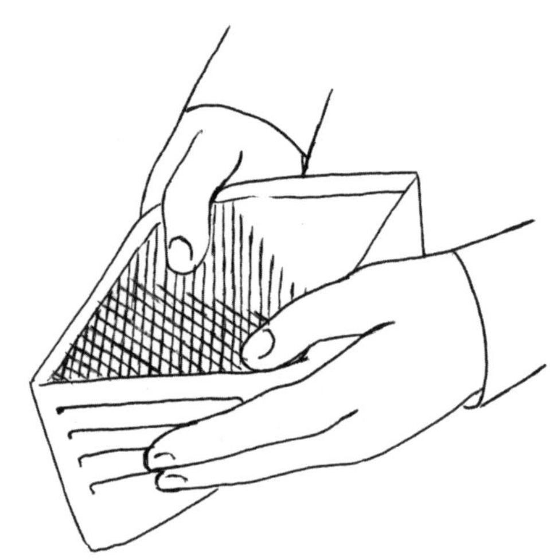

محفظة

wallet

(der) Geldbeutel

24/02

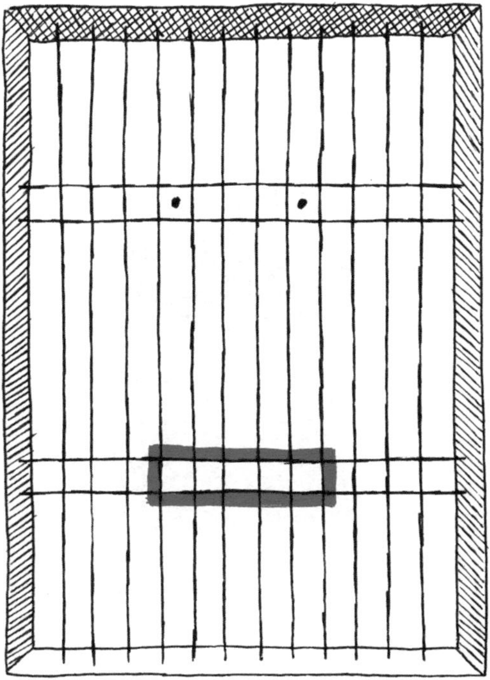

سجن

jail

(das) Gefängnis

25/02

نيء

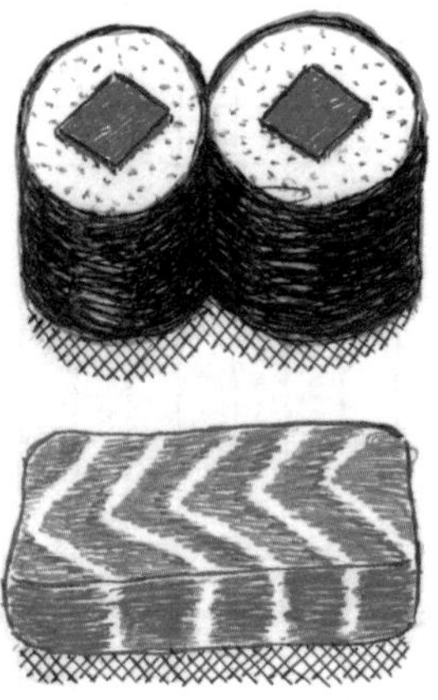

raw

roh

26/02

حوض الاستحمام

bathtub

(die) Badewanne

تنكّر

disguise

(die) Verkleidung

28/02

أخطبوط

octopus

(die) Krake

ورق الجدران

wallpaper

(die) Tapete

إمساك

constipation

(die) Verstopfung

03/03

أبكم

mute

stumm

04/03

سميك

thick

dick

05/03

تكرار

repetition

(die) Wiederholung

ببغاء

parrot

(der) Papagei

جسر الأسنان

dental bridge

(die) Zahnbrücke

08/03

يوم المرأة العالمي

International Women’s Day

(der) Weltfrauentag

09/03

شارب

mustache

(der) Schnurrbart

10/03

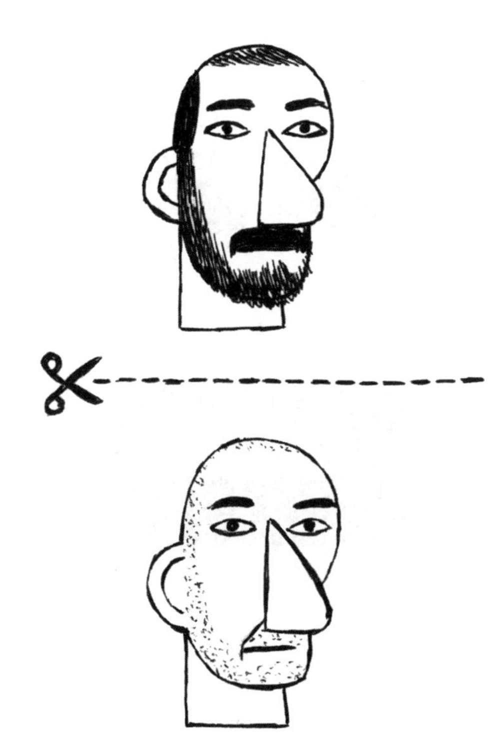

تحوّل

metamorphosis

(die) Verwandlung

11/03

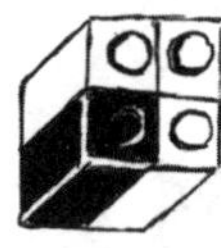

حجر البناء

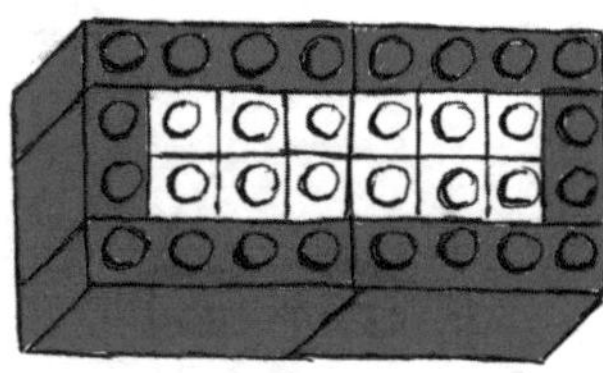

building block

(der) Baustein

12/03

طفولي

childish

kindisch

13/03

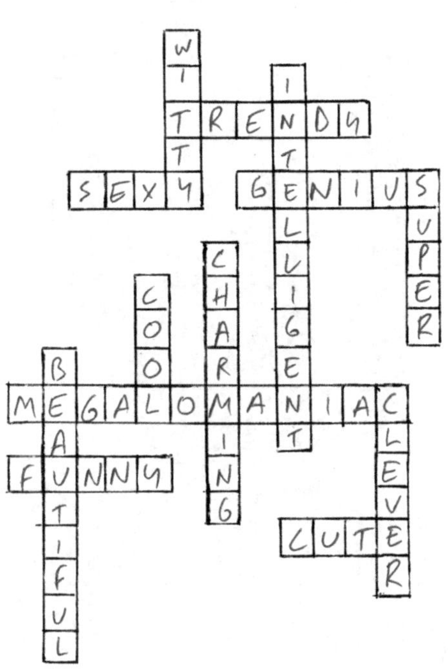

crossword

كلمات متقاطعة

(das) Kreuzworträtsel

14/03

مصاب بجنون العظمة

megalomaniac

größenwahnsinnig

15/03

عائلة ملكيّة

royal family

(die) Königsfamilie

16/03

بطل

hero

(der) Held

17/03

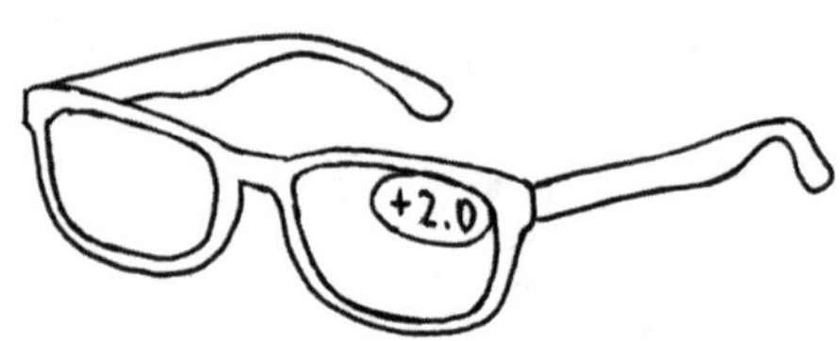

تقدّم في السن

aging

(das) Altern

18/03

piggy bank

(das) Sparschwein

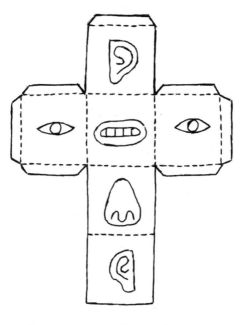

Cut on solid lines. Fold on dashed lines.

فن تكعيبي

Cubism

(der) Kubismus

20/03

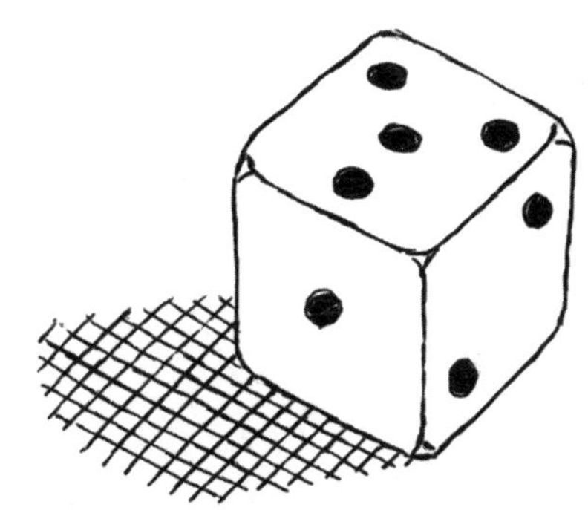

نرد

dice

(der) Würfel

21/03

بداية الربيع

beginning of spring

(der) Frühlingsanfang

22/03

حرف

letter

(der) Buchstabe

23/03

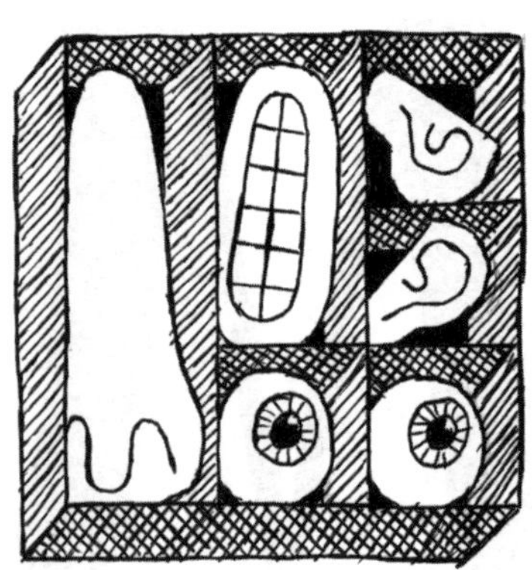

to tidy up

aufräumen

24/03

يستمع

to listen

lauschen

25/03

جامع الأشياء

collector

(der) Sammler

26/03

جذور

ECONOMY

KERBAGE / MAZEN
BERLIN TXL
BEIRUT
JU 355 Y 26 MAR
20:45
C84 20115 2C NO

PLD 0044 MMTXL
ET KT 11570775263

roots

(die) Wurzeln

27/03

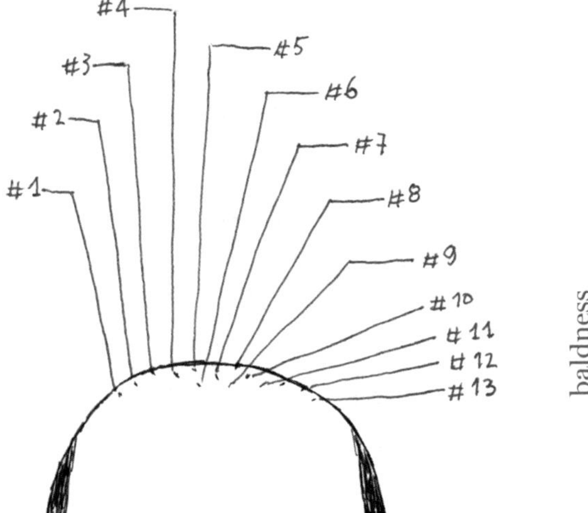

baldness

(die) Kahlheit

28/03

liar

(der) Lügner

29/03

رسم تخطيطي

sketch

(die) Skizze

30/03

هويّة شخصيّة

ID card

(der) Personalausweis

31/03

يتجاوز

to walk past

vorübergehen

01/04

بيضة عيد الفصح

Easter egg

(das) Osterei

02/04

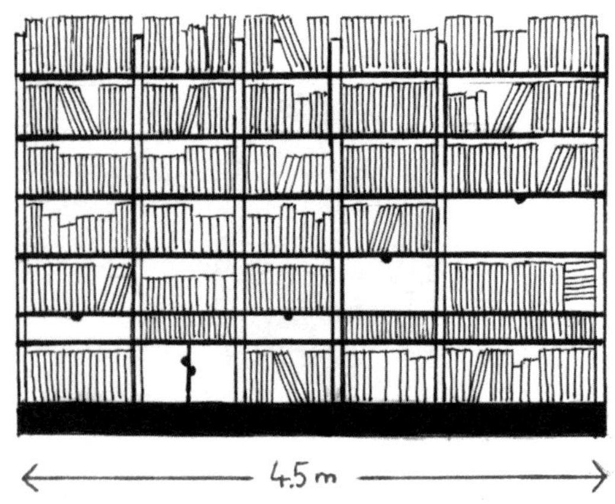

ثروة

wealth

(der) Reichtum

قدر

fate

(das) Schicksal

04/04

parent's house

(das) Elternhaus

05/04

حداد

mourning

(die) Trauer

06/04

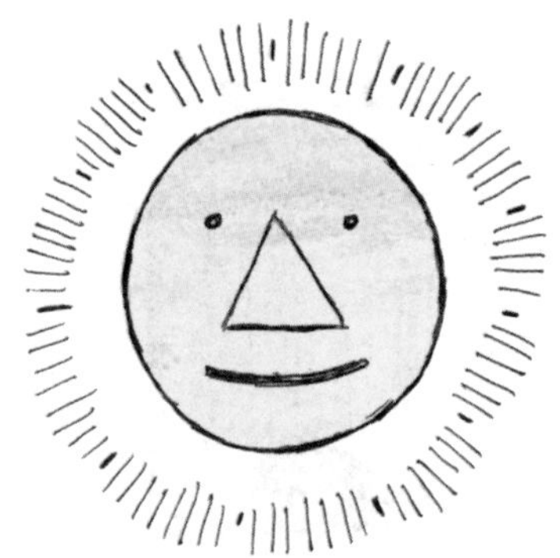

نور الشمس

sunshine

(der) Sonnenschein

07/04

to sweat

schwitzen

عطلة عائليّة

family holiday

(der) Familienurlaub

09/04

صاروخ

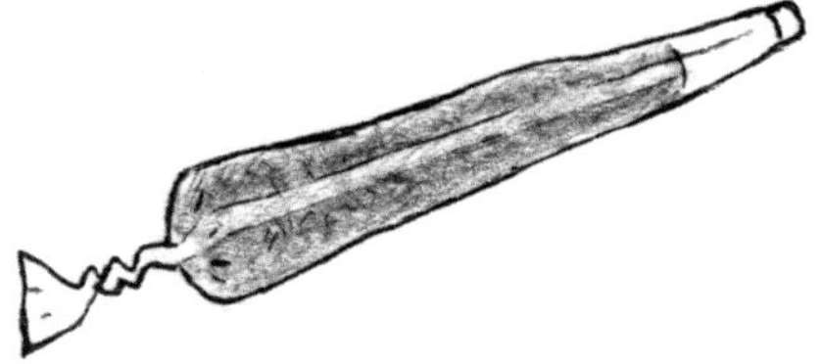

rocket

(die) Rakete

10/04

TODAY, i WILL NOT
MAKE A DRAWING.

قرار

decision

(die) Entscheidung

11/04

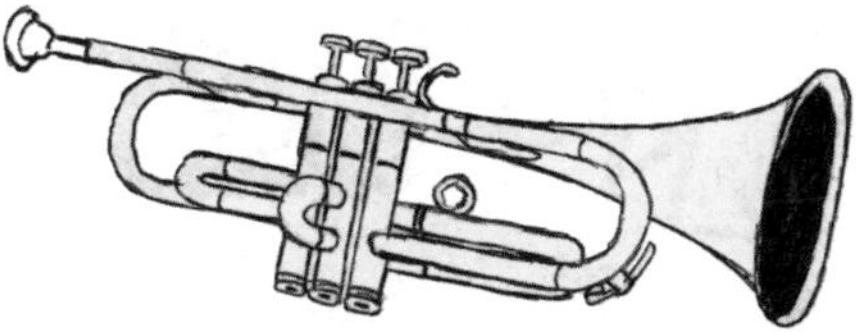

breathing filter

(der) Atemfilter

embarrassing

peinlich

13/04

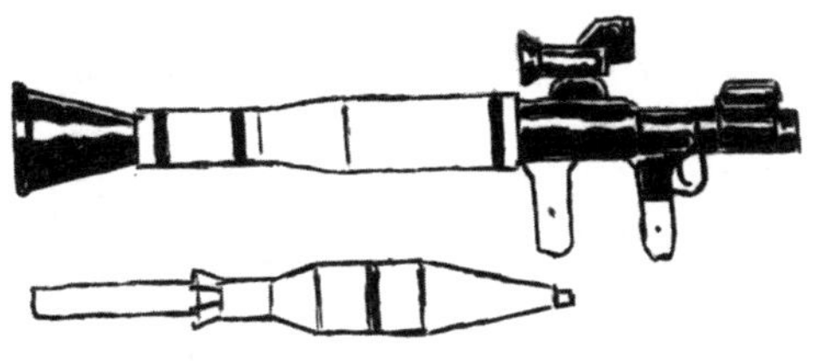

ذكرى

commemoration

13 APRIL 1975

Beginning of the Lebanese civil war

(das) Gedenken

14/04

سكران

drunk

betrunken

Ich bin

Ich bin
Bin ich?
Was bin ich?
Ich bin Fass

Mazen Rimbaud

قصيدة

poem

16/04

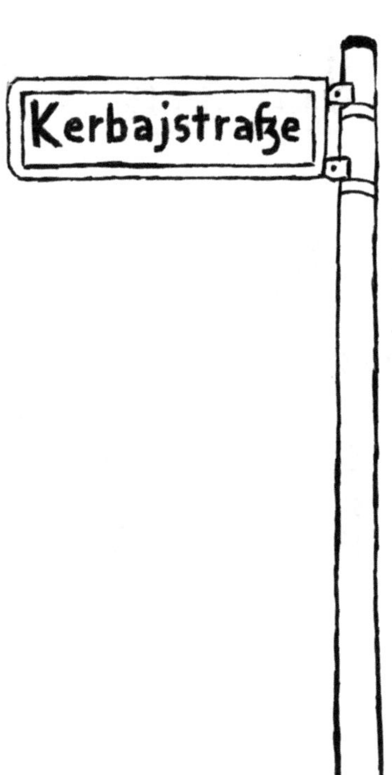

street name

(der) Straßenname

نباتي

vegetarian

vegetarisch

18/04

وشم

tattoo

•

(forearm)

(die) Tätowierung

19/04

كرة الديسكو

disco ball

(die) Diskokugel

20/04

tower

(der) Turm

كتاب الكائنات الخفيّة

hidden picture book

(das) Wimmelbuch

22/04

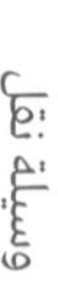

means of transport

(das) Transportmittel

23/04

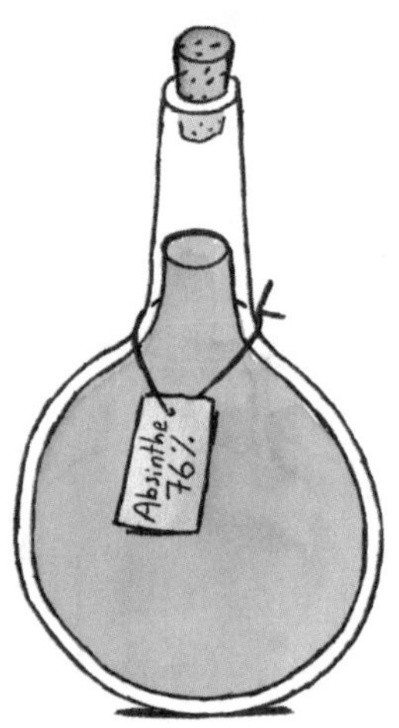

magic potion

(der) Zaubertrank

24/04

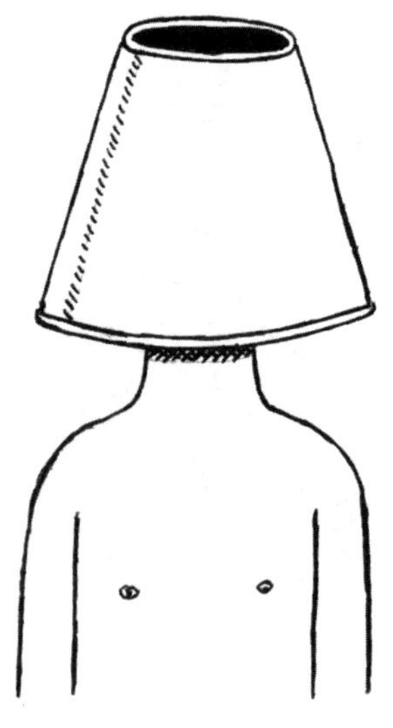

نعامة

ostrich

(der) Strauß

25/04

مبسّط

simplified

vereinfacht

26/04

ضفدع الطين

toad

(die) Kröte

27/04

قصة في القصة

story within a story

(die) Schachtelgeschichte

28/04

ممحي

erased

ausradiert

crazy idea

(die) Schnapsidee

30/04

دليل المستخدم

user’s manual

(der) Benutzerhandbuch

SPOT THE DIFFERENCE

تغيير

change

1998

2018

(die) Veränderung

02/05

أحجية

puzzle

(das) Rätselspiel

03/05

مشهور

famous

berühmt

03/05

sleepy

schläfrig

ينظّم

to put in order

ordnen

06/05

secret weapon

(die) Geheimwaffe

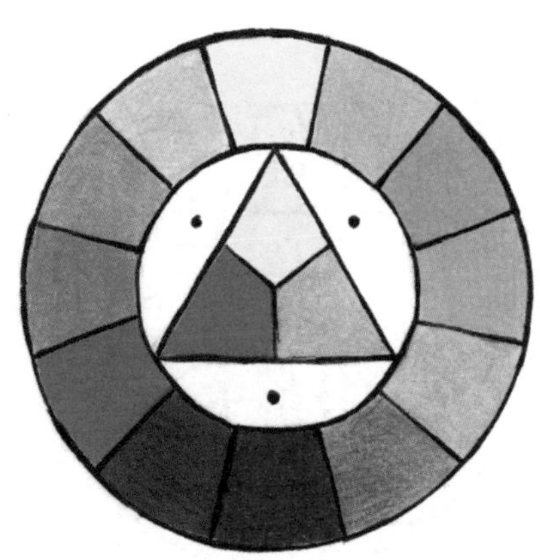

دولاب الألوان

color wheel

(der) Farbkreis

08/05

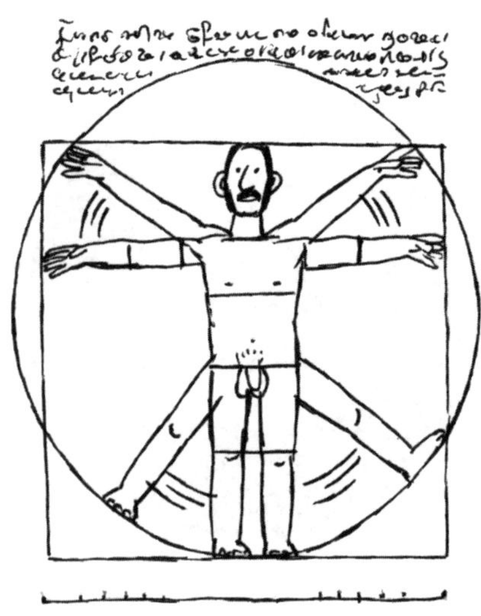

movement

(die) Bewegung

09/05

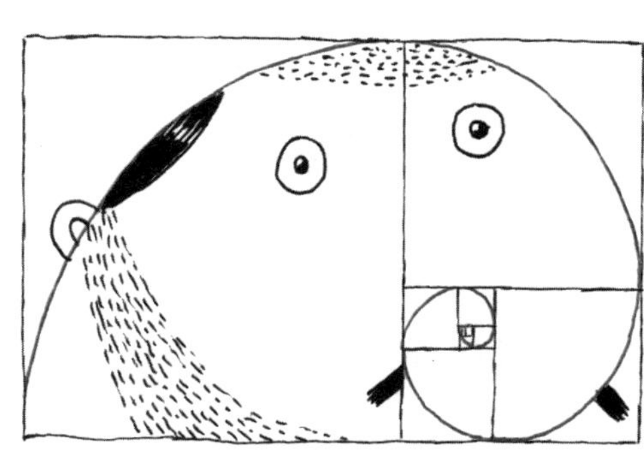

نسبة

proportion

(das) Verhältnis

10/05

ORDER NOW from headache-comics.com

ALSO AVAILABLE: Vol. 1 & Vol. 2

تسويق الذات

self-promotion

(die) Eigenwerbung

11/05

طريق ذو اتجاه واحد

one-way street

(die) Einbahnstraße

12/05

تجاري

commercial

kommerziell

13/05

دقيق

punctual

pünktlich

14/05

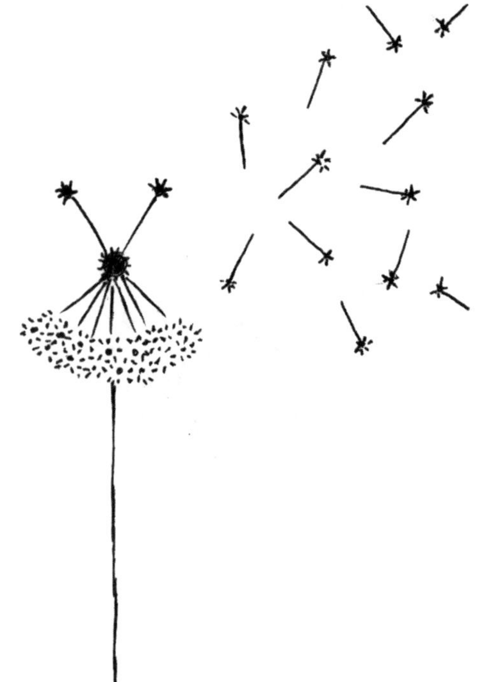

هندباء

dandelion

(die) Pusteblume

15/05

دمى متحرّكة

hand puppet

(die) Handpuppe

16/05

seemingly dead

scheintot

17/05

علم المصريّات

Egyptology

(die) Ägyptologie

18/05

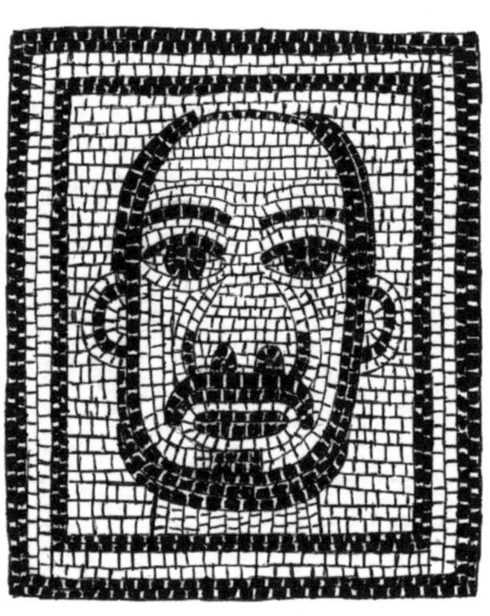

حجارة الموزاييك

mosaic tiles

(die) Mosaikfliesen

19/05

سرعة

velocity

(die) Geschwindigkeit

20/05

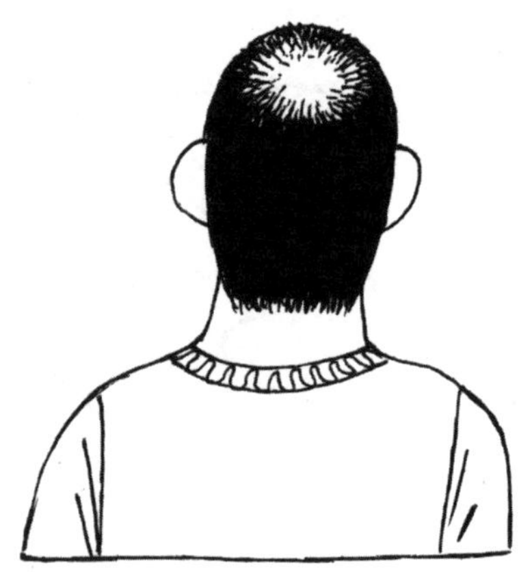

rear view

(die) Rückansicht

21/05

ظل

shadow

(der) Schatten

22/05

بارع في استخدام كلتا يديه

ambidextrous

beidhändig

ظرف

envelope

(der) Umschlag

24/05

منتهك

(self-portrait by Alex Baladi)

usurper

(der) Thronräuber

25/05

I will not let someone else do my daily drawing.

I will not let someone else do my daily drawing.

I will not let someone else do my daily drawing.

I will not let someone else do my daily drawing.

I will not let someone else do my daily drawing.

I will not let someone else do my daily drawing.

I will not let someone else do my daily drawing.

عقوبة

punishment

(die) Strafe

26/05

مغنّي السول

soul singer

(der) Soulsänger

27/05

خرية

shit

(die) Kacke

28/05

reverse shot

(die) Gegenaufnahme

INFORMATION SHEET

Name MAZEN

Surname KERBAJ

Sex MALE

Date of birth 24/08/75

Marital status MARRIED

Names and dates of birth of children

EVAN KERBAJ - 04/02/01

ALIA KERBAJ - 14/07/09

NOUR KERBAJ - 14/07/09

خصوبة

fertility

(die) Fruchtbarkeit

30/05

كيس القمامة

trash bag

(der) Müllsack

31/05

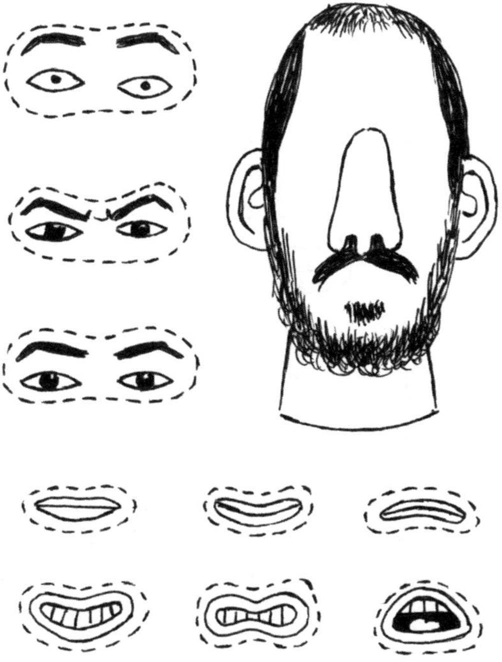

facial expression

(der) Gesichtsausdruck

01/06

مالك

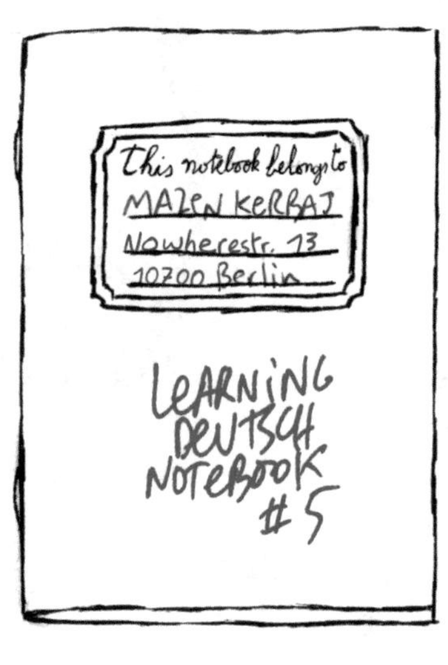

owner

(der) Inhaber

02/06

degenerate

entartet

03/06

أجنبي

foreigner

(der) Ausländer

صندوق إعادة التدوير

recycling bin

(die) Wertstofftonne

حلوى الدببة

gummy bear

(das) Gummibärchen

06/06

punctuation marks

(die) Satzzeichen

07/06

رياضة شعبيّة

popular sport

(der) Volkssport

08/06

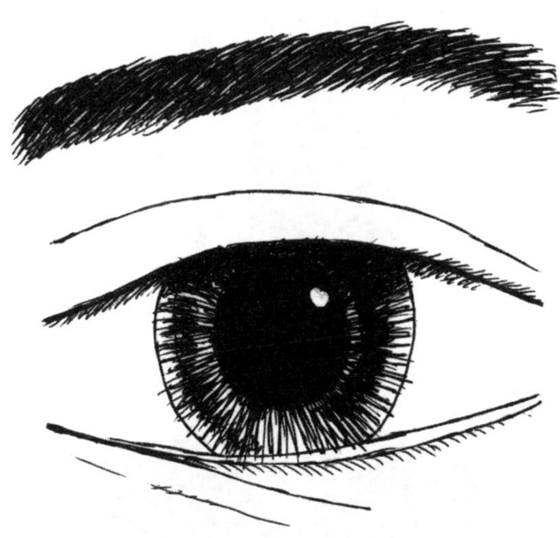

صورة مقرّبة

close-up

(die) Nahaufnahme

09/06

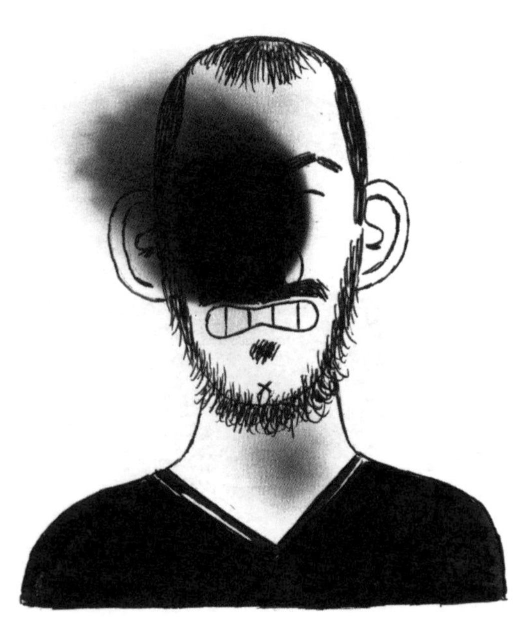

محروق

burnt

verbrannt

10/06

أداة

device

(das) Gerät

11/06

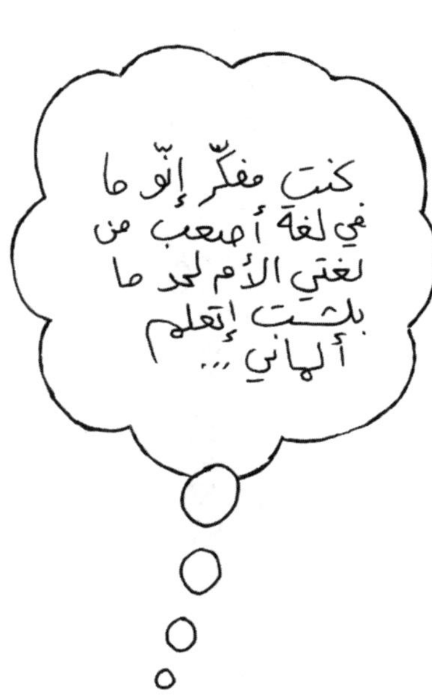

اللغة الأم

mother tongue

(die) Muttersprache

12/06

أحلام وهميّة

pipe dream

(das) Luftschloss

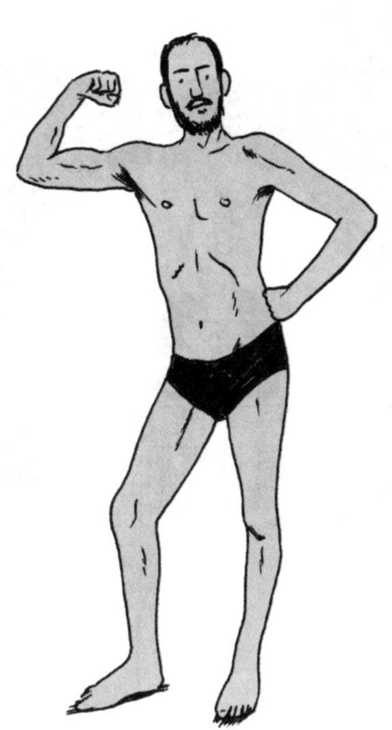

كمال الأجسام

body building

(der) Muskelaufbau

14/06

secret agent

(der) Geheimagent

15/06

عرّاف

fortune teller

(der) Wahrsager

16/06

مكان النزهة

picnic spot

(der) Picknickplatz

17/06

هدف

target

(die) Zielscheibe

18/06

زيادة الوزن

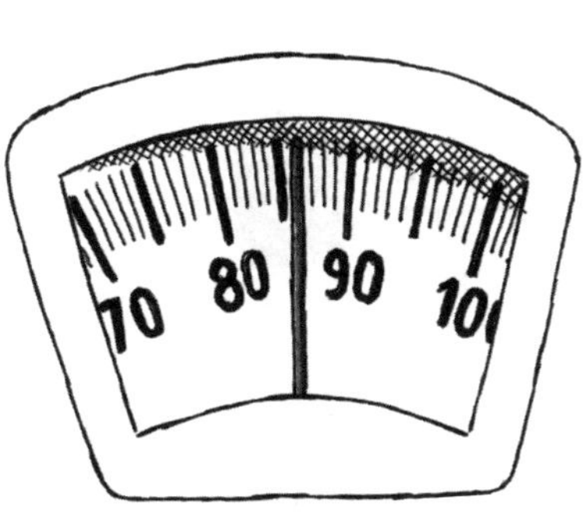

weight gain

(die) Gewichtszunahme

19/06

مروحة كهربائية

electric fan

(der) Lüfter

20/06

pixelated

verpixelt

سلام

peace

(der) Frieden

آلة لوحة المفاتيح

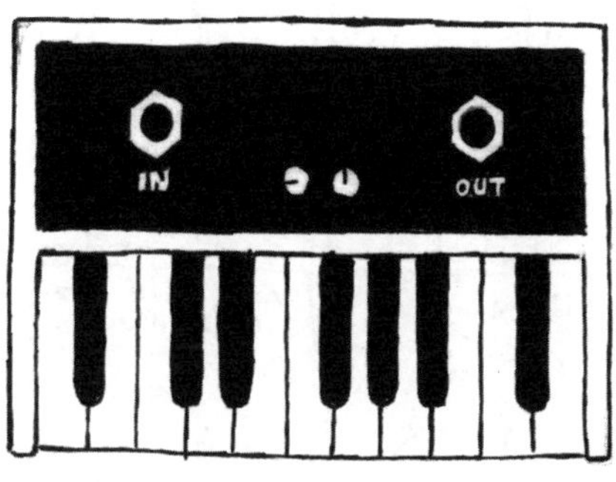

keyboard instrument

(das) Tasteninstrument

23/06

متسلسل

sequential

sequenziell

24/06

عشّاق

lovers

(die) Liebenden

25/06

مخاط

snot

(der) Rotz

26/06

cult of personality

(der) Personenkult

27/06

مضخم الصوت

amplifier

(der) Verstärker

28/06

ذكرى الزواج

wedding anniversary

(der) Hochzeitstag

29/06

إسهال

diarrhea

(der) Durchfall

30/06

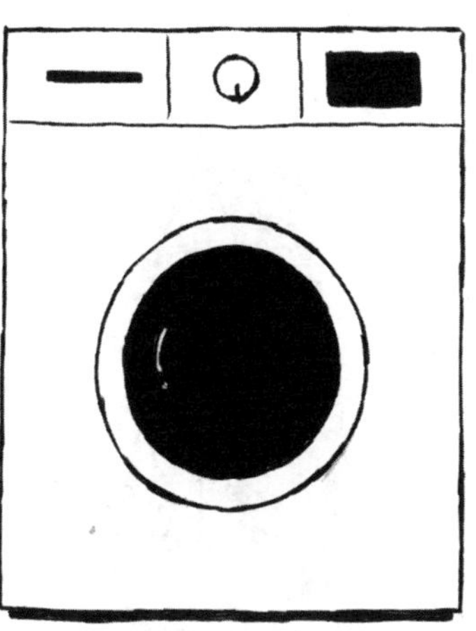

houshold electronics

(die) Unterhaltungselektronik

01/07

رجل الكهف

prehistoric man

(der) Urmensch

02/07

حلزون

snail

(die) Schnecke

03/07

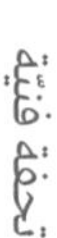

masterpiece

(das) Meisterwerk

04/07

ستنسل

stencil

(die) Schablone

فن الشارع

street art

(die) Straßenkunst

ذات الرداء الأحمر

Little Red Riding Hood

(das) Rotkäppchen

07/07

مترامن

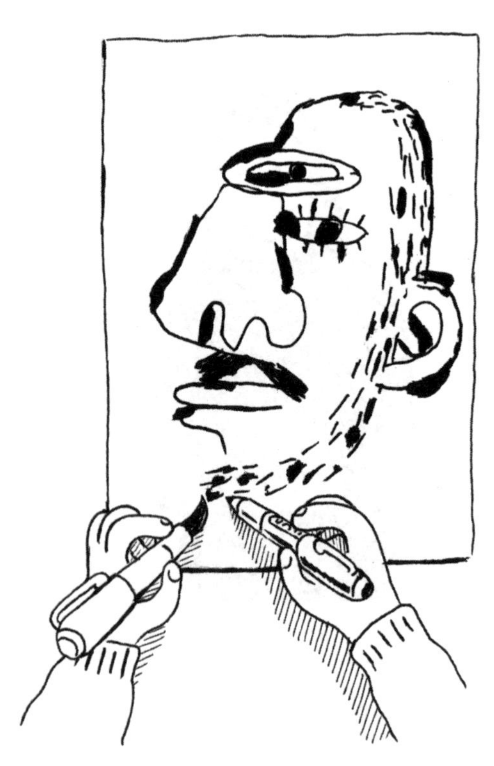

simultaneous

gleichzeitig

08/07

unique

einzigartig

09/07

أحمر الشفاه

lipstick

(der) Lippenstift

10/07

فزّاعة

scarecrow

(die) Vogelscheuche

11/07

mechanical

mechanisch

12/07

روزنامة المناسبات

events calendar

(der) Veranstaltungskalender

قائمة المهام

to-do list

(die) Aufgabenliste

خوف من الطيران

fear of flying

(die) Flugangst

15/07

hometown

(die) Heimatstadt

16/07

عطلة صيفيّة

summer holidays

(die) Sommerferien

17/07

عوّامة

buoy

(die) Boje

18/07

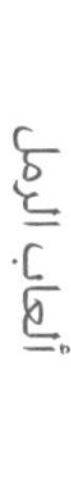

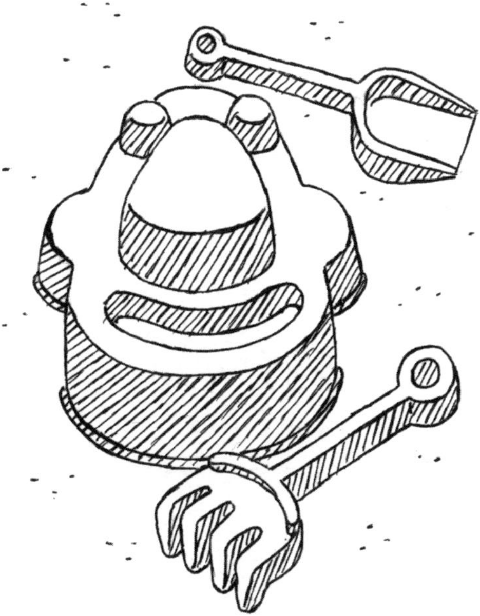

sand toys

(das) Sandspielzeug

ذوب

to melt

schmelzen

20/07

air conditioner

(die) Klimaanlage

21/07

pool

(das) Schwimmbecken

22/07

سعادة

happiness

(das) Glück

23/07

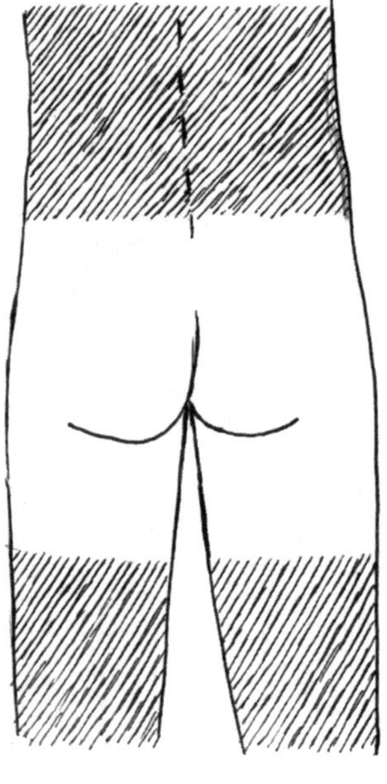

إسمرار

suntan

(die) Bräune

24/07

زي تقليدي

traditional costume

(die) Tracht

25/07

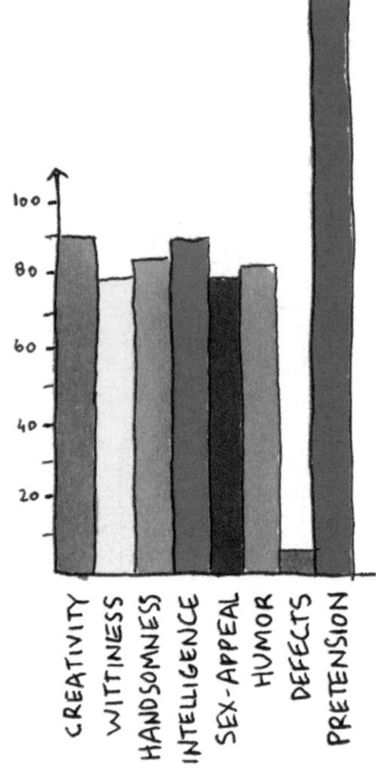

رسم بياني

chart

(die) Grafik

26/07

لا نهاية

infinity

(die) Unendlichkeit

27/07

cyclops

(der) Zyklop

28/07

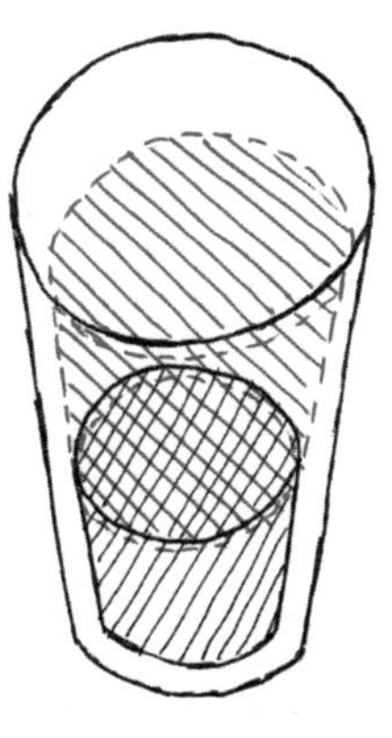

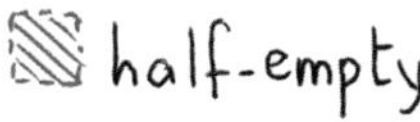

متردد

undecided

unentschieden

29/07

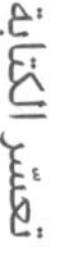

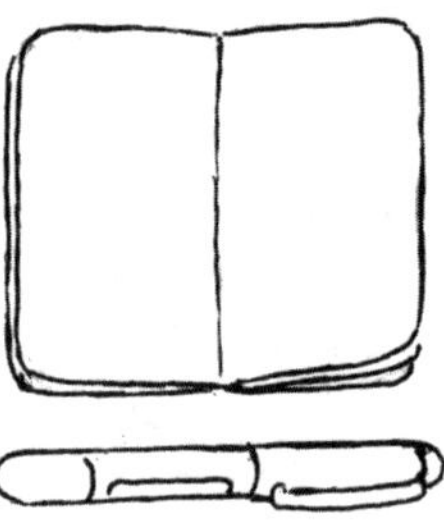

writer's block

(die) Schreibblockade

30/07

حمامة

pigeon

(die) Taube

31/07

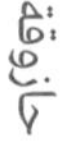

hiccups

(der) Schluckauf

01/08

كلام الناس

word-of-mouth

(die) Mundpropaganda

02/08

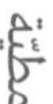

mount

(das) Reittier

تلخيص

Mazen Kerbaj is an artist and musician born in Beirut in 1975 and living in Berlin since 2015.
His works include *Learning Deutsch*, a project initiated in 2018, where he learns a new German word every day and draws a related self-portrait.

summary

(die) Zusammenfassung

04/08

صديق صالح

good friend

(der) Duzfreund

يشخر

to snore

schnarchen

06/08

روتين يومي

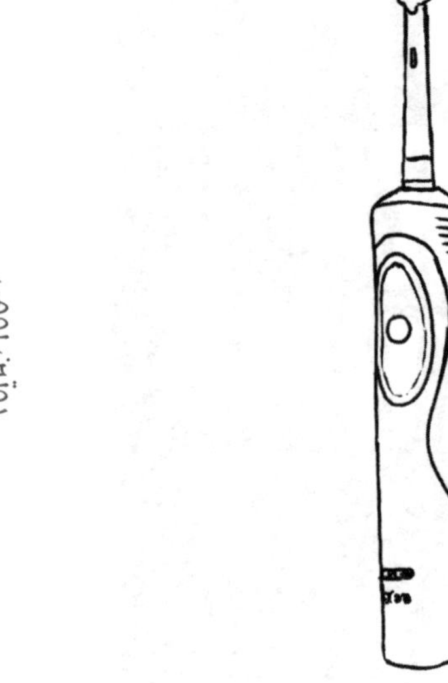

daily routine

(die) Tagesroutine

مروحة

fan

(der) Fächer

08/08

مكبّر الصوت

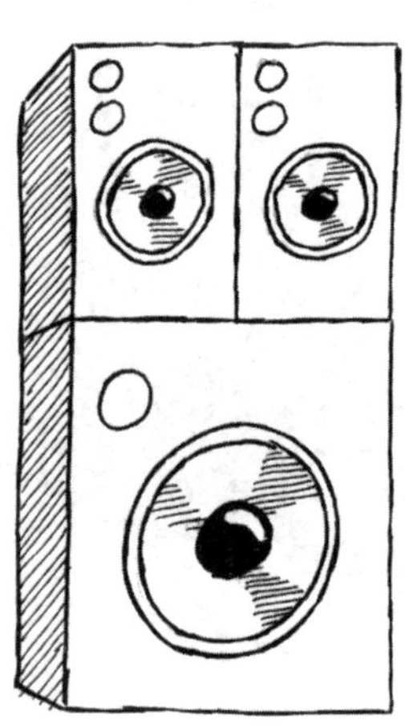

loudspeaker

(der) Lautsprecher

09/08

مجنون الحفلات

party animal

(der) Partylöwe

10/08

مألوف

familiar

vertraut

11/08

دائم

durable

dauerhaft

12/08

معدّات

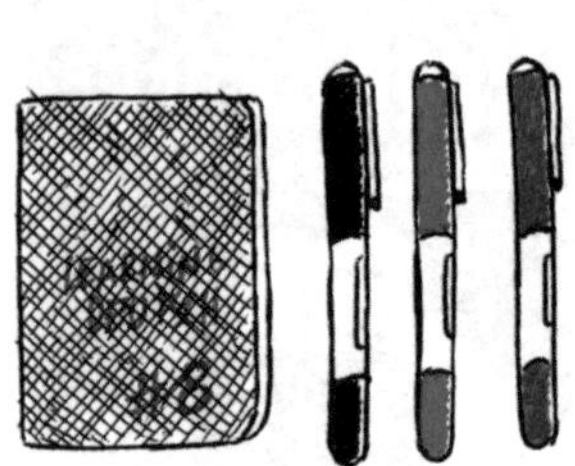

equipment

(die) Ausrüstung

13/08

معداد

counting frame

(der) Abakus

14/08

حورية البحر

mermaid

(die) Meerjungfrau

15/08

مشروب ما قبل النوم

nightcap

(der) Absacker

16/08

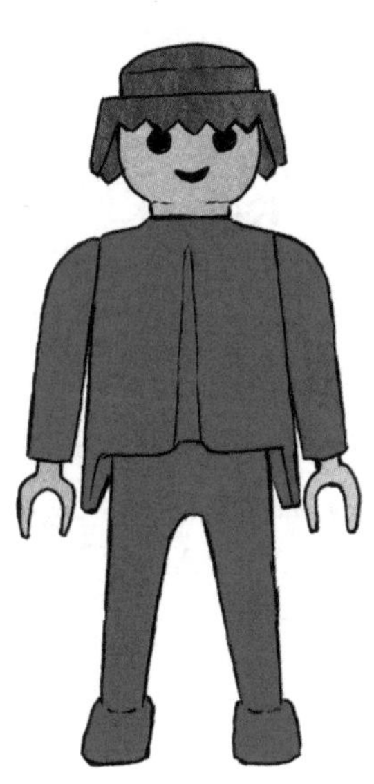

ذكريات الطفولة

childhood memories

(die) Kindheitserinnerungen

17/08

يشاهد التلفاز

to watch television

fernsehen

18/08

متحذلق

know-it-all

(der) Besserwisser

19/08

لسعة النحلة

bee sting

(der) Bienenstich

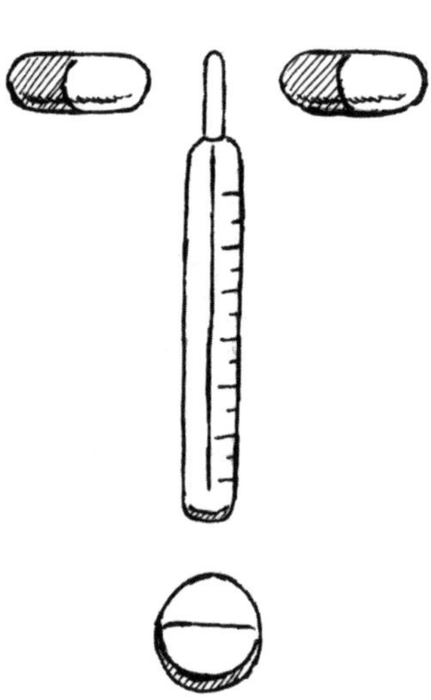

محموم

feverish

fiebrig

21/08

طريق سريع

expressway

(die) Schnellstraße

22/08

بيت متنقّل

mobile home

(das) Wohnmobil

23/08

ازدحام

congestion

(der) Stau

24/08

شموع عيد الميلاد

birthday candles

(die) Geburtstagskerzen

25/08

ناقص

missing

fehlend

26/08

ورق اللعب

deck of cards

(das) Kartenspiel

27/08

يخادع

to bluff

bluffen

ساحرة

witch

(die) Hexe

29/08

بعيد

far

weit

30/08

منظر

view

(der) Ausblick

31/08

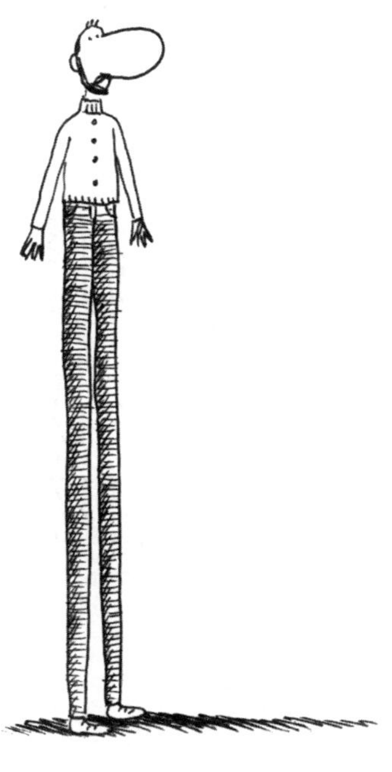

مبالغة

exaggeration

(die) Übertreibung

01/09

traitor

(der) Verräter

THIS PROJECT WAS MADE POSSIBLE THANKS TO:

AND: MIDORI NOTEBOOK

فاصل إعلاني

commercial break

(der) Werbeblock

03/09

رهبة المسرح

stage fright

(das) Lampenfieber

04/09

بقرة

COW

(die) Kuh

05/09

today's date

(das) Tagesdatum

شريحة

slice

(die) Scheibe

07/09

شعر مستعار

wig

(die) Perücke

08/09

يستيقظ

to wake up

aufwachen

09/09

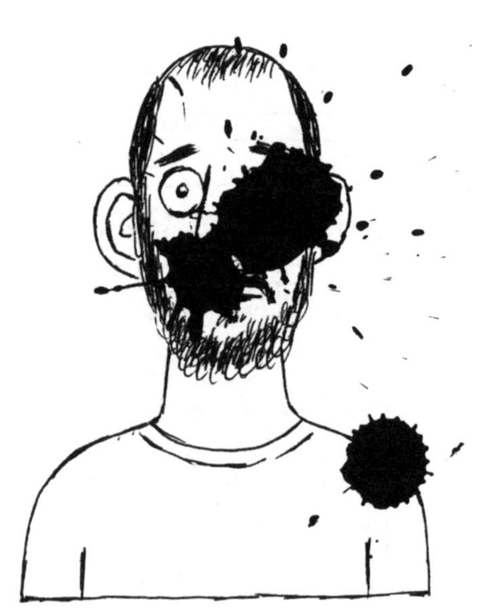

أخرق

clumsy

ungeschickt

10/09

مراقبة

surveillance

(die) Überwachung

بخار

steam

(der) Dampf

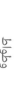

12/09

bat

(die) Fledermaus

13/09

T. May

J. Besos

V. Putin

K. Kardashian

D. Trump

B.H. Levy

A. Khaminei

H. Weinstein

M. Zuckerberg

معاصرون

contemporaries

(die) Zeitgenossen

14/09

كتاب مفضّل

favorite book

(das) Lieblingsbuch

15/09

نسخة طبق الأصل

replica

(die) Nachbildung

16/09

نبيل

nobleman

(der) Edelmann

17/09

خطم

snout

(die) Schnauze

18/09

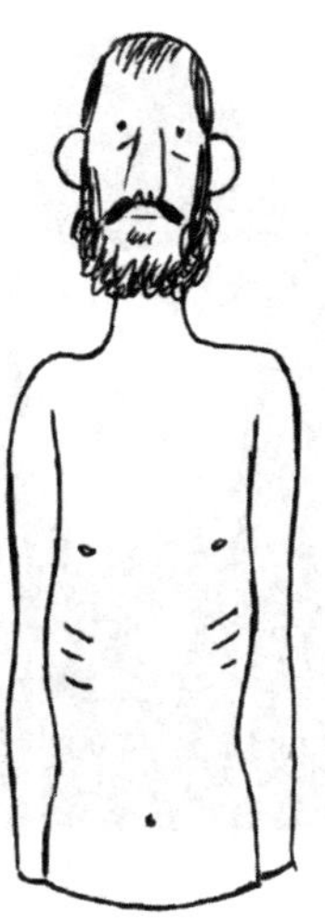

نحيف

thin

mager

19/09

قلنسوة

hoody

(der) Kapuzenpullover

عملية تجميل الأنف

nose job

(die) Nasenkorrektur

21/09

عسر القراءة

dyslexia

(die) Legasthenie

22/09

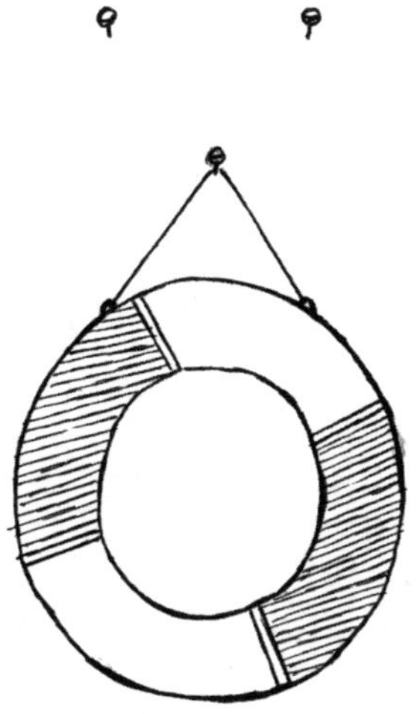

طوق النجاة

lifebelt

(der) Rettungsring

23/09

REST OF THE WORLD

MAZEN

REST OF THE WORLD

0 25 50 75 100

حدود

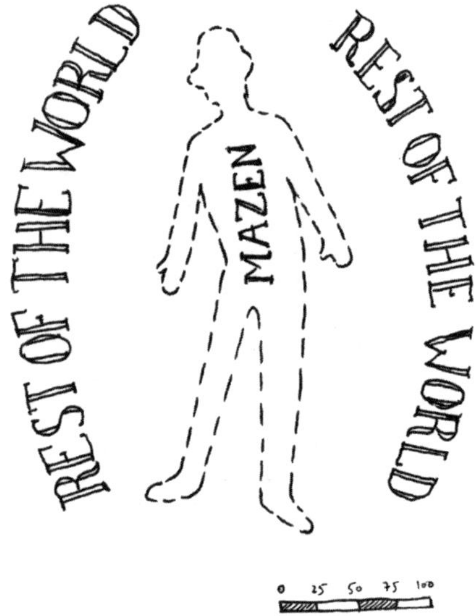

border

(die) Grenze

24/09

تاريخ انتهاء الصلاحيّة

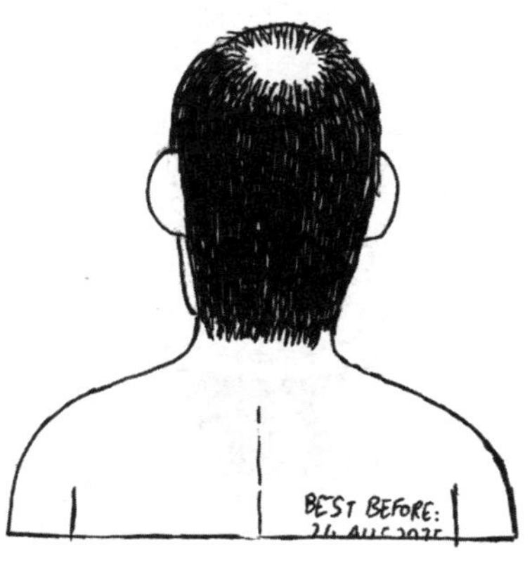

expiration date

(das) Verfallsdatum

25/09

كرة أرضيّة

globe

(die) Erdkugel

26/09

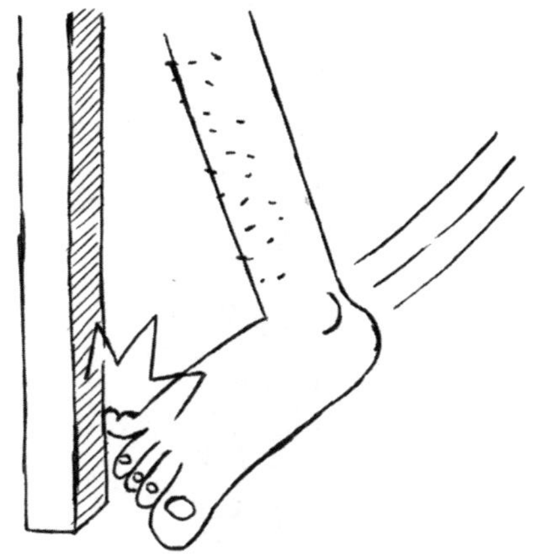

آخ!

ouch!

aua!

27/09

ورق العنب

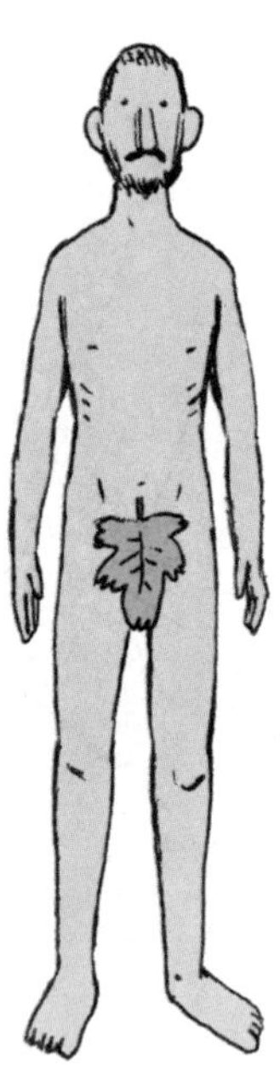

vine leaf

(das) Weinblatt

28/09

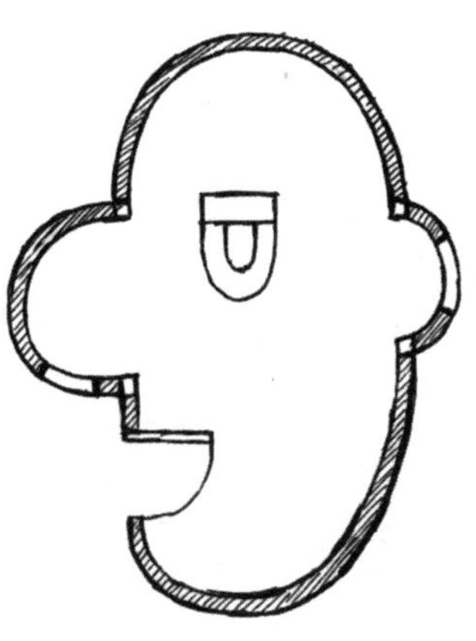

مخطط الطابق

floor plan

(der) Grundriss

29/09

shower curtain

(der) Duschvorhang

30/09

خطأ مطبعي

printing error

(der) Druckfehler

01/10

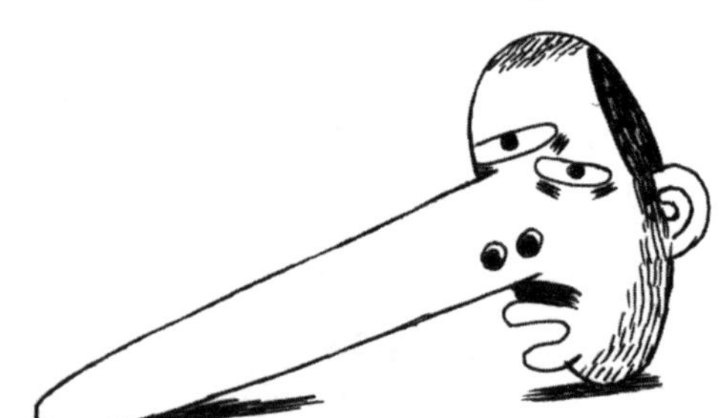

to lie

lügen

02/10

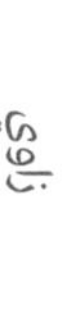

angular

eckig

محّار

oyster

(die) Auster

باقة الزهور

bouquet of flowers

(der) Blumenstrauß

05/10

ثنائي الجنس

hermaphrodite

(der) Zwitter

06/10

مبالغ فيه

overrated

überbewertet

thinker

(der) Denker

حمّالة الصدر

bra

(der) Büstenhalter

ناضج

ripe

reif

ضباب

fog

(der) Nebel

11/10

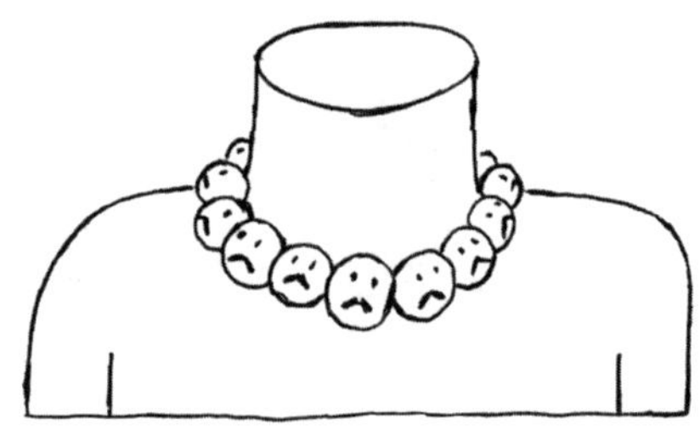

عقد

necklace

(die) Halskette

12/10

مصارع السومو

sumo wrestler

(der) Sumoringer

13/10

weightlifter

(der) Gewichtheber

14/10

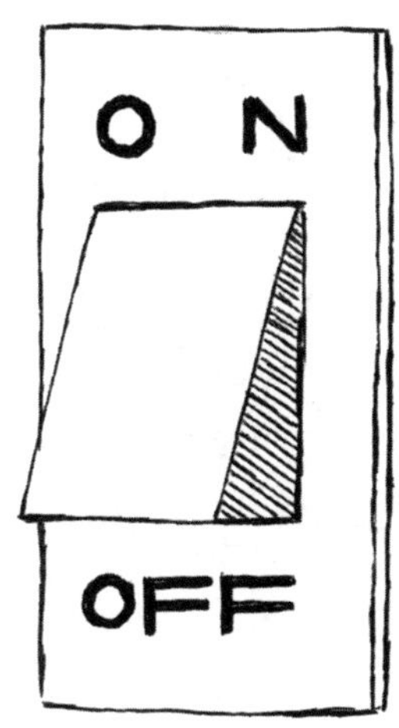

switch

(der) Schalter

15/10

wrinkled

faltig

16/10

to iron

bügeln

17/10

mindfulness meditation

(die) Achtsamkeitsmeditation

18/10

مضرب كرة الريشة

badminton racket

(der) Federballschläger

19/10

جزيرة القيامة

Easter Island

(die) Osterinsel

20/10

ستائر

blinds

(die) Jalousien

21/10

عظمة الساق

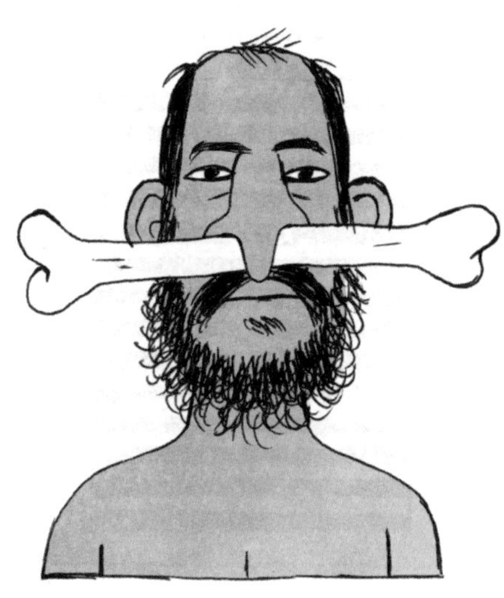

tibia

(das) Schienbein

22/10

أدوات الرسم

drawing tools

a. Pen

b. Brush

c. Nib

(das) Zeichenwerkzeug

23/10

نكاشة القطن

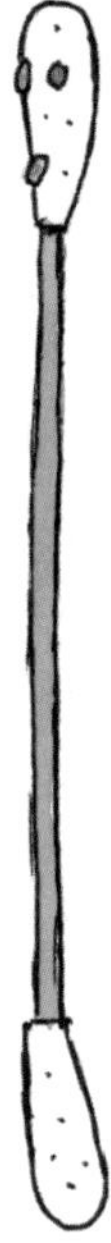

cotton swab

(das) Wattestäbchen

24/10

صخرة

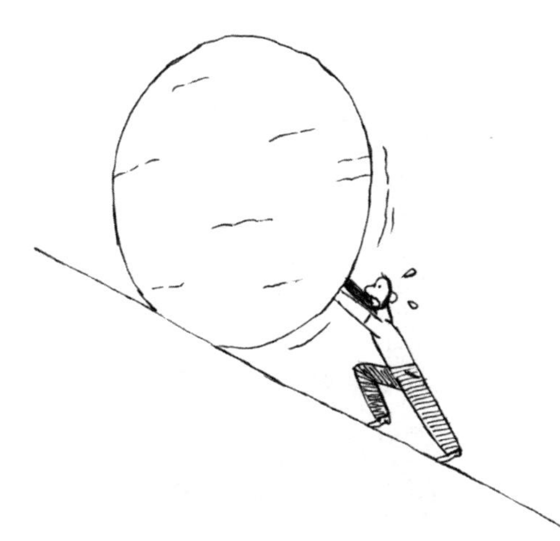

rock

(der) Felsbrocken

25/10

علبة الكبريت

matchbox

(die) Streichholzschachtel

26/10

فقاعة الكلام

speech bubble

(die) Sprechblase

27/10

كائن فضائي

alien

(der) Außerirdische

فرجار

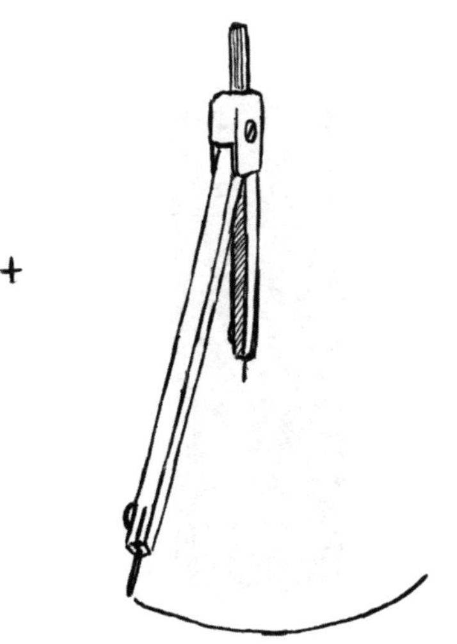

compass

(der) Zirkel

29/10

remote control

(die) Fernbedienung

30/10

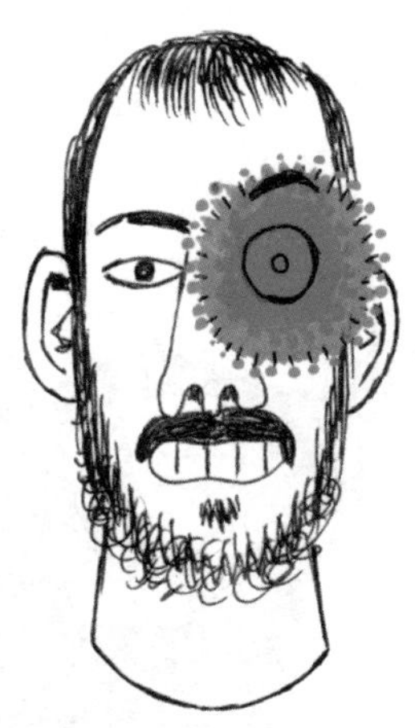

إشارة الانعطاف

turn signal

(der) Blinker

مخيف

scary

unheimlich

مهدد بالانقراض

endangered

gefährdet

مجعد

curly

lockig

03/11

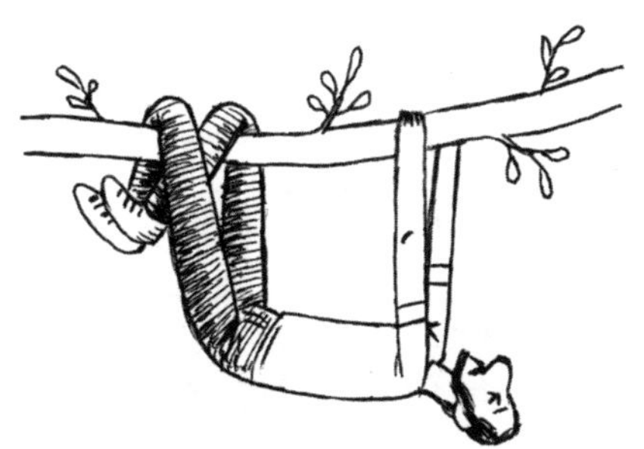

حيوان الكسلان

sloth

(das) Faultier

غروب الشمس

sunset

(der) Sonnenuntergang

05/11

حيوان محشو

cuddly toy

(das) Kuscheltier

06/11

صنم

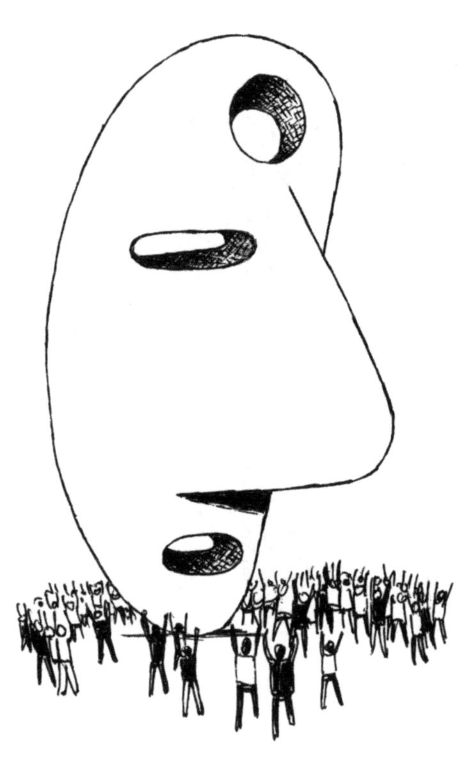

idol

(das) Götzenbild

07/11

ينوّم مغناطيسياً

to hypnotize

hypnotisieren

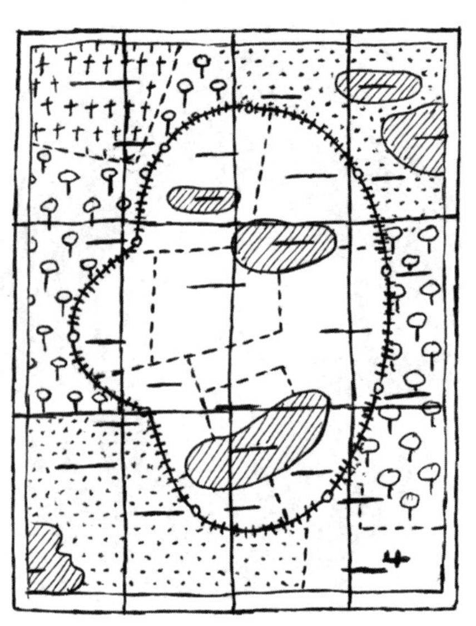

خريطة المدينة

city map

(der) Stadtplan

09/11

بطاقة العمل

business card

(die) Visitenkarte

10/11

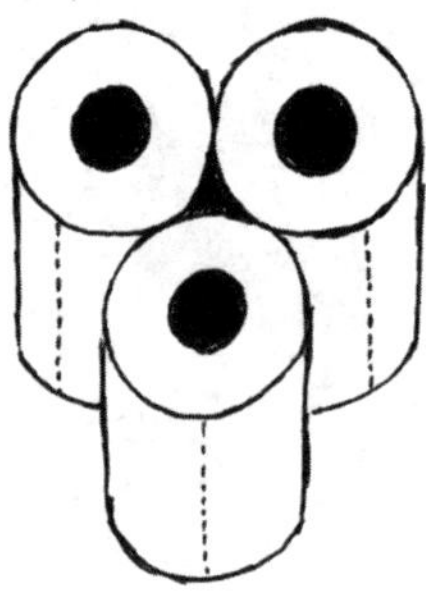

ورق الحمام

toilet paper

(das) Toilettenpapier

11/11

memory

(die) Erinnerung

12/11

مفرقعات ناريّة

firecracker

(der) Feuerwerkskörper

تحيك

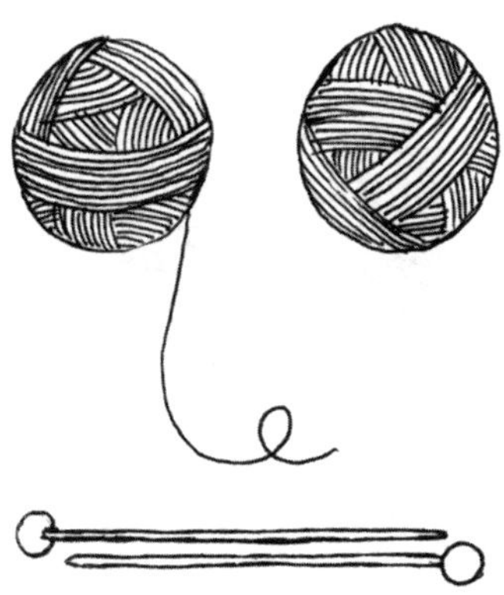

to knit

stricken

14/11

hedgehog

(der) Igel

15/11

مصارع

wrestler

(der) Ringer

مقطوع الرأس

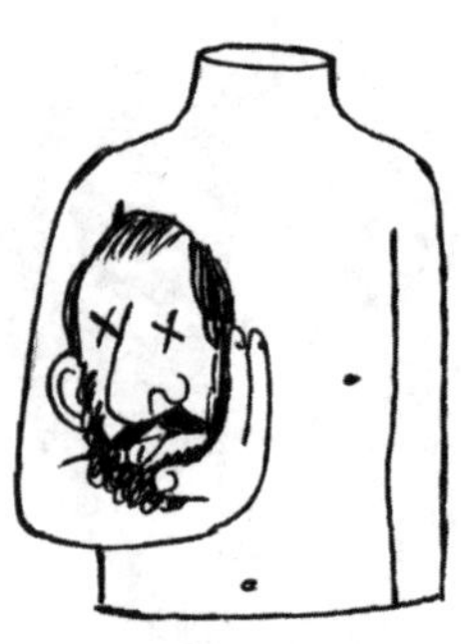

beheaded

enthauptet

17/11

قطرة

drop

(der) Tropfen

18/11

برغي

screw

(die) Schraube

19/11

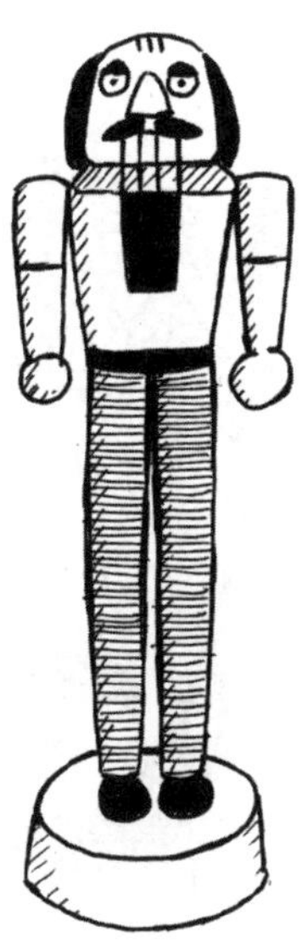

كسّارة البندق

nutcracker

(der) Nussknacker

20/11

تهوية

aeration

(das) Belüften

أدوات

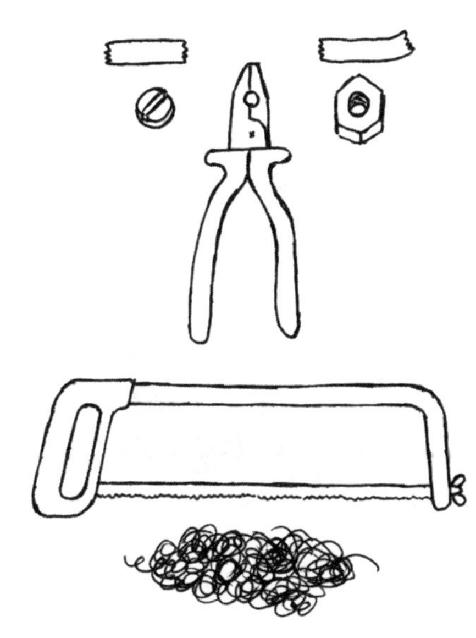

tools

(das) Werkzeug

22/11

لا غنى عنه

indispensable

unentbehrlich

بركة

puddle

(die) Pfütze

24/11

كائن ليلي

nocturnal

nachtaktiv

25/11

سنفور

smurf

(der) Schlumpf

26/11

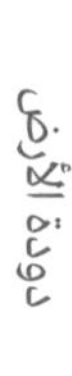

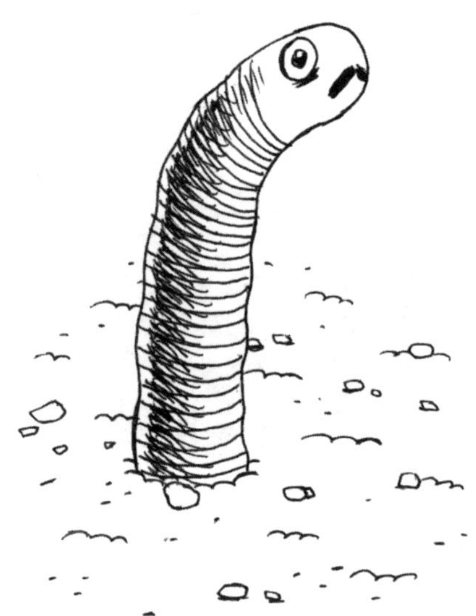

earthworm

(der) Regenwurm

27/11

- ☐ Continue to read the book I am reading
- ☐ Take a nap
- ☐ Vacuum the living-room
- ☐ Go for a walk
- ☐ Watch the news
- ☐ Make my daily drawing

يماطل

to procrastinate

aufschieben

28/11

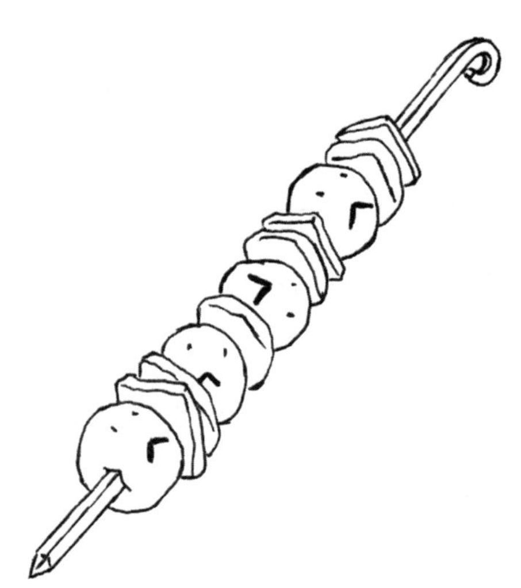

سيخ

skewer

(der) Spieß

29/11

seven-league boots

(die) Siebenmeilenstiefel

30/11

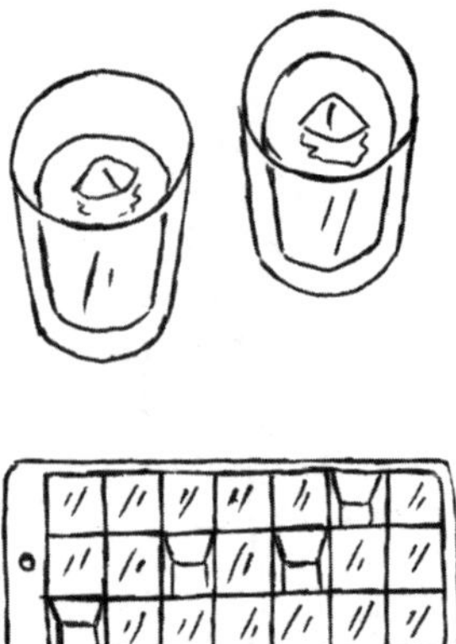

مكعّبات الثلج

ice cube

(der) Eiswürfel

01/12

إكليل من ورق

paper garland

(die) Papiergirlande

02/12

مشنوق

hung

aufgehängt

03/12

autumn leaves

(das) Herbstlaub

04/12

خرطوم

hose

(der) Schlauch

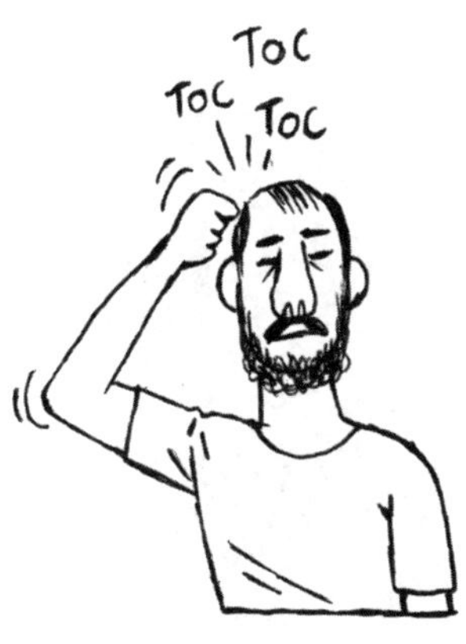

يقرع

to knock

klopfen

06/12

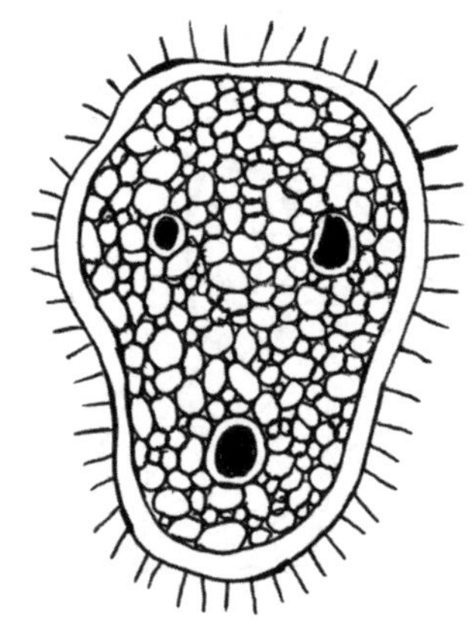

أميبا

amoeba

(die) Amöbe

رموش

eyelashes

(die) Wimpern

08/12

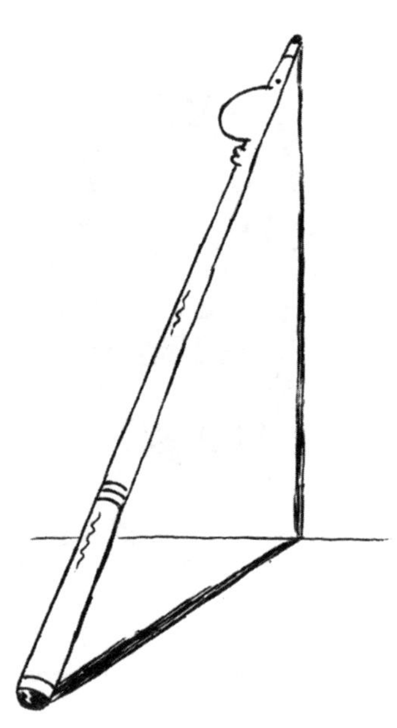

عصا البلياردو

billiard cue

(das) Billardqueue

09/12

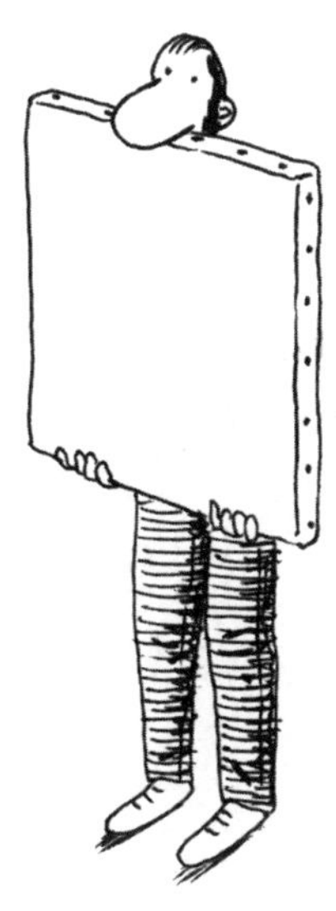

حامل

easel

(die) Staffelei

10/12

غبار

dust

(der) Staub

11/12

wooden figure

(die) Holzfigur

دانتيل

lace

(die) Spitze

13/12

موسم عيد الميلاد

Christmas season

(die) Weihnachtszeit

14/12

منشار كهربائي

chainsaw

(die) Kettensäge

15/12

رجل الثلج

snowman

(der) Schneemann

تعذيب

torture

(die) Folter

17/12

أحادي القرن

unicorn

(das) Einhorn

18/12

تنين

dragon

(der) Drache

19/12

رجل خبز الزنجبيل

gingerbread man

(der) Lebkuchenmann

20/12

(der) Weihnachtsbaumschmuck

Christmas tree decoration

زينة شجرة الميلاد

21/12

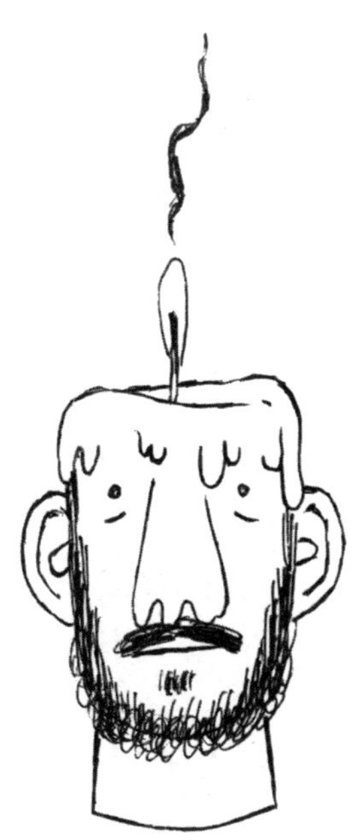

candle

(die) Kerze

22/12

saline bag

(der) Infusionsbeutel

23/12

قارض

rodent

(das) Nagetier

عشاء عيد الميلاد

Christmas dinner

(das) Weihnachtsessen

25/12

سخيف

ridiculous

lächerlich

26/12

سائق سيّارة الأجرة

taxi driver

(der) Taxifahrer

27/12

رقص تقليدي في مناطق بفاريا

traditional dance from Bavaria

(der) Schuhplattler

28/12

مدبرة المنزل

housemaid

(die) Haushälterin

29/12

مضحك

funny

ulkig

نبوءة

prophecy

(die) Prophezeiung

31/12

خلاص

deliverance

(die) Befreiung

LEARNING DEUTSCH

Edited by Mazen Kerbaj and Racha Gharbieh
Designed by Mazen Kerbaj and Studio Safar

Project manager: Anna Warnow
Production: Thomas Lemaître
Paper: Munken Lynx Rough
Printing: Graspo CZ, a.s.

A big thank you to:
Burkhard Beins, Tony Buck, Vesna Chamoun, Nour Flayhan, Julia Gerlach, Ahmad Gharbieh, Racha Gharbieh, Laure Ghorayeb, Nick Grindell, Albrecht Hotz, Hatem Imam, Alia, Nour and Evan Kerbage, Andrew Lafkas, Cristina Marx, Caline Matar, Magda Mayas, Mani Pournaghi, Konrad Siller, Michael Thieke, Silke Urban, Nicola von Velsen, Michael Vorfeld, Ute Wassermann, and everyone who followed the project on social media and suggested new words or corrections.

A very special thank you to Alex Baladi for the marvelous drawing of 24.05.2018

Published by
Hatje Cantz Verlag GmbH
Mommsenstraße 27
10629 Berlin
www.hatjecantz.com

A Ganske Publishing Group Company

ISBN 978-3-7757-5638-9

Printed in the Czech Republic